After The Alphabet

A Two Letter Word Primer

PRISTINE
PRESS AND MEDIA

RICHHI ROSS

After The Alphabet: A Two Letter Word Primer
Copyright © 2025 by Richhi Ross

ISBN
978-1-969642-15-9 (Paperback)
978-1-969642-14-2 (eBook)
978-1-969642-16-6 (Hardcover)

Dedicated to Orion Richhi Ross

I AM

AN apple

AS new
AS gold

AT home

AW cute

BE good

BY now

DO right

GO ahead

HA HA

HE smiled

what IF

IN here

IS hot

love IT

MA MA

hug ME

MY dog

piece OF

OR else

blue OX

PA PA

SO big

TO market

UP stairs

with US

WE sing

www.ingramcontent.com/pod-product-compliance
Lightning Source LLC
Chambersburg PA
CBHW041131120626
46547CB00019B/2941